The Story of
Johnny Appleseed

written and illustrated by **Aliki**

Simon and Schuster Books for Young Readers
Published by Simon & Schuster Inc., New York

Many years ago
when America was a new country,
there lived a brave and gentle man
named John Chapman.
John loved the out-of-doors.
He would walk for miles
in the woods
among the trees and the flowers,
happy and alone with his thoughts.

Published by Simon and Schuster Books for Young Readers
A Division of Simon & Schuster, Inc.
1230 Avenue of the Americas
New York, NY 10020

20   19   18   17   16   15   14

10   pbk

Simon and Schuster Books for Young Readers
is a trademark of Simon & Schuster, Inc.
Manufactured in the United States of America

Library of Congress Catalog Card Number: 63-8507
ISBN 0-671-66298-8
ISBN 0-671-66746-7

One day, after a long walk,
John sat under a tree to rest.
He felt the warm sun on his back,
and the fresh grass tickling his toes.
John took an apple from his sack
and ate it.
And when he had finished,
he looked in his hand
at what was left—
just a few brown seeds.
And John thought:
If one gathered seeds,
and planted them,
our land would soon be filled
with apple trees.

John Chapman lived on the frontier,
in Massachusetts,
where the country had been settled.
But every day pioneers were
leaving to travel west,
where there were no homes
or villages and where
the only roads were Indian trails.

In their covered wagons,
the pioneers made the long
and dangerous journey
through the wilderness.
They wanted to build
new lives for themselves
in a new part of the country.
John Chapman went, too.
But he did not travel in
a covered wagon.
He walked in his bare feet.
He carried no weapons,
as men did in those days,
to protect themselves
from wild animals and danger.
He carried only a large sack
on his back,
filled with apple seeds,
and his cooking pan
on his head.

As he walked,
John planted seeds.
He gave a small bagful
to everyone he saw.
Soon, everyone who knew him
called him Johnny Appleseed.

Sometimes Johnny stopped
for many weeks,
helping the pioneers.
They cleared the land.
They built homes.
They planted rows and rows
of apple trees.
When they were finished,
Johnny walked on to help others.
But he always came back
to see his friends.

Everyone loved Johnny Appleseed,
especially the children.
When Johnny rested from his planting,
the children sat around him,
listening to all his adventures.

Johnny Appleseed walked alone.
He slept out of doors,
in the woods
or by the river
He met wolves and foxes,
birds and deer.
They were all his friends.

One day, as Johnny was eating lunch,
he heard a noise,
and three little bear cubs
ran from behind a tree.
When the mother bear came
and saw them playing together,
she sat and watched.
She knew Johnny Appleseed
would not harm her young.

Johnny met many Indians
on the way.
He was kind to them
and gave them seeds and herbs,
which they used as medicine.
Although the Indians were not friendly
to any white men
who chased them from their homes,
Johnny was their friend.

Johnny did not like people to fight.
He tried to make peace
between the settlers and the Indians,
for he believed that all
men should live together as brothers.

On and on Johnny walked,
planting as he went.
When he needed more seeds,
he collected sackfuls
from the cider mills.
Everyone saved his apple seeds
for Johnny.
Many years passed.
Johnny Appleseed walked on.
He visited his friends,
and saw with pleasure
the many apple trees
which covered the land.
And he was happy.

But then, one year,
there was a long, cold winter.
When spring should have come,
snow was still on the ground,
and frost was on the trees.
Johnny could not sleep or eat.
He was afraid his trees
would die.

As he was walking
among the trees one day,
Johnny Appleseed fell to the ground.
He was very ill.
After some hours,
an Indian mother and her son passed
and saw Johnny lying in the cold.
Quickly the boy ran for help.
Johnny was carried to their village,
not far away.

For many days he lay ill with fever.
The Indians gave him medicine
and nursed him.

And one day, Johnny Appleseed
opened his eyes.
He smiled at his Indian friends.
He knew they had saved his life.
He saw that the sun was warm,
and the frost had left the trees.
Spring had come at last,
and Johnny was well again.
But he never forgot his friends
and went to see them often.

Johnny Appleseed,
the gentle pioneer,
lived for many years,
planting apple trees
wherever he went.
We can still see them today.
They are large and old
and heavy with apples.
They are the gift Johnny Appleseed
gave to his country,
and to you and to me.